DATE DUE

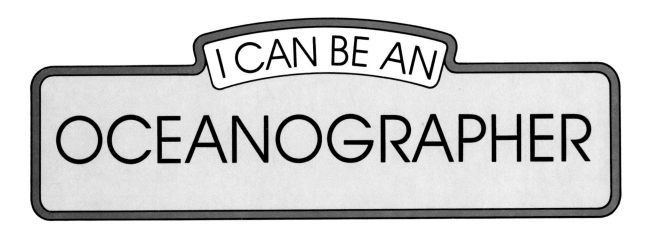

I CAN BE AN
OCEANOGRAPHER

By Paul P. Sipiera

Prepared under the direction of Robert Hillerich, Ph.D.

 CHILDRENS PRESS ®

CHICAGO

Library of Congress Cataloging-in-Publication Data
Sipiera, Paul P.

  I can be an oceanographer.

  Includes index.
  Summary: Discusses the work oceanographers do as
they study the ocean's depths.
  [1. Oceanographers. 2. Occupations] I. Title.
GC30.5.S56   1987   551.46'0023   86-31006
ISBN 0-516-01905-8

Childrens Press, Chicago
Copyright ©1987 by Regensteiner Publishing Enterprises, Inc.
All rights reserved. Published simultaneously in Canada.
Printed in the United States of America.
  2 3 4 5 6 7 8 9 10 R 96 95 94 93 92 91 90 89 88 87

PICTURE DICTIONARY

oceans

oceanographer

deep sea mining

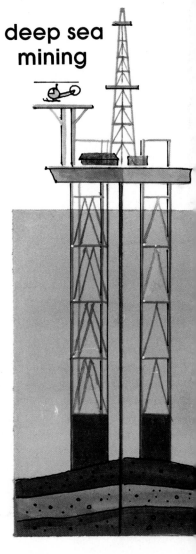

research vessel

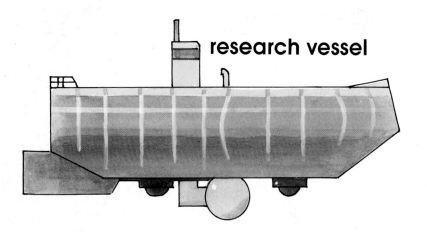

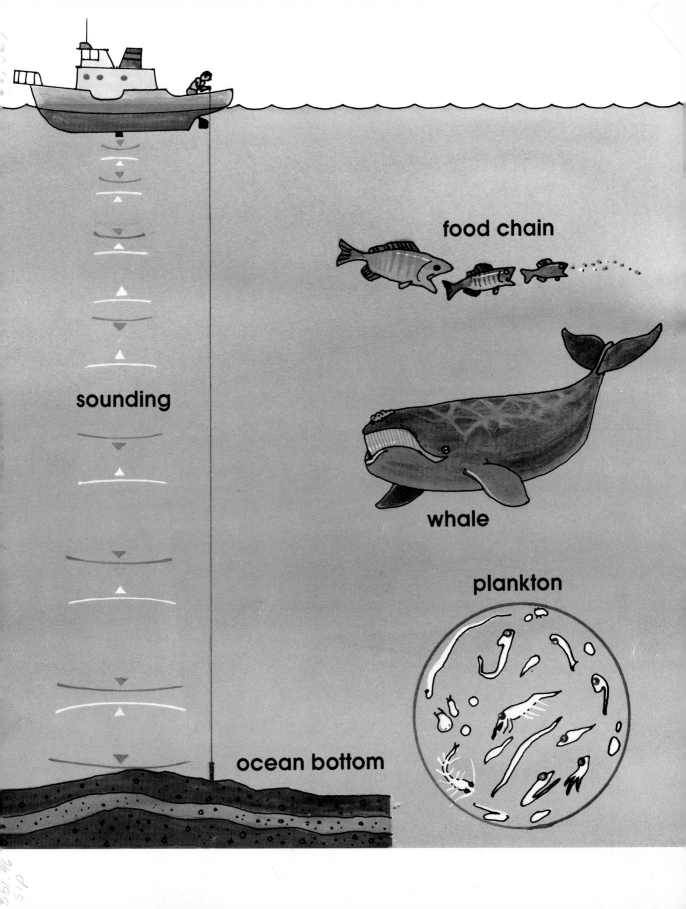

food chain

sounding

whale

plankton

ocean bottom

Above: A photo of the planet Earth, taken from space
Below: Tides along the California seashore

Look at a photograph of the planet Earth taken from space. What do you see? Over 70 percent of our planet is covered by oceans. Scientists who study the oceans are called oceanographers.

oceans

Oceanographers study all aspects of the sea, from observing fish to measuring the daily rise and fall of the tides.

oceanographer

In diving vessels such as this one, oceanographers can study deep-sea life.

Oceanographers
carefully study how the
atmosphere, the land,
and the oceans interact.
The oceans are very
important to life on Earth.
Oceans are home for
millions of fish and

Some inhabitants of the oceans: Top—White jack; a dolphin
Bottom—Dwarf herring; an elephant seal

mammals. Animals on
land depend on the
oceans for food and
oxygen, too. The oceans
even control our weather.
Without the oceans,

The diving vessel *Deepstar,* inside the cabin (left) and on its way down (right)

almost all life on Earth would die.

Oceanographers study the oceans by using many different kinds of instruments. Their principal tool is the research vessel.

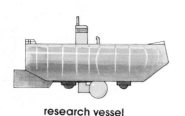

research vessel

Sea laboratories operated by the
Department of the Navy. The *Trieste* is at left.

From these ships, scientists
can collect fish for study
or explore the ocean
bottom. Deep diving
vessels such as the *Trieste*
have taken scientists to
the ocean's greatest
depths.

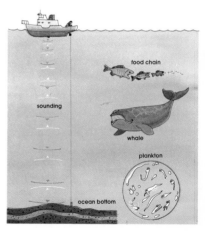

ocean bottom

9

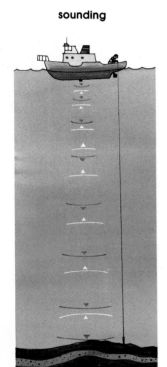

sounding

To measure how deep the ocean is, oceanographers "take a sounding." They may do this simply by dropping a line with a weight on the end until it hits bottom.

A more modern way is to use an echo sounder. An echo sounder can measure depth and also map the ocean bottom. It sends out a pulse of sound that travels from

SCRIPPS SEA BEAM SYSTEM

A printout of the ocean floor (left). It was produced by an instrument called Sea Beam, aboard the research vessel *Thomas Washington* (right).

the surface to the ocean bottom, and back to the surface again. By measuring how long it takes the sound to travel, oceanographers know how deep the ocean is in that spot.

A diver studies a fish called a sea raven.

Oceanographers called marine biologists study the fish and mammals that live in the ocean. Too much fishing and hunting in the sea can cause serious

problems. The food chain
in the oceans must remain
unbroken. All living things
depend upon one another.
If one species dies out,
this could cause the death
of many more.

food chain

A killer whale off the coast of
Flordia (above) and a shark (right)

whale

plankton

Many large sea
animals, such as some
whales and sharks,
depend upon
microscopic creatures
called plankton for food.
Certain species of whales
depend on a shrimp-like
creature called krill as

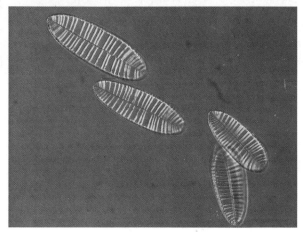

Diatoms (left top and bottom) are among the many types of microscopic organisms that make up plankton. Krill (above) are tiny, shrimp-like creatures eaten by whales and other sea animals.

their source of food. Over-fishing of krill could cause those species to die. Oceanographers must constantly watch fish catches to keep a balance in nature.

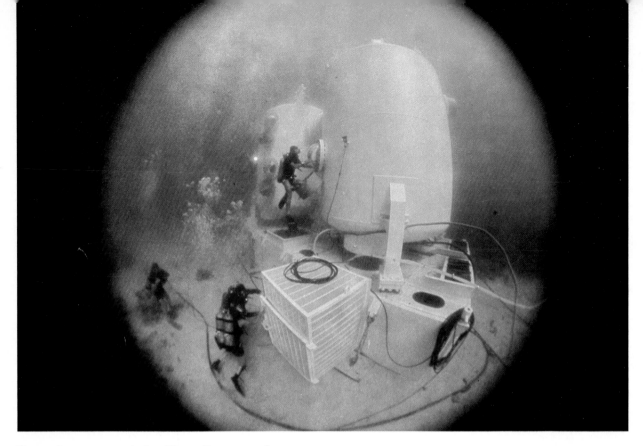

These divers are exploring life on the ocean floor,
using their research vessel as a base of operation.

The marine biologist
also studies creatures
living deep in the ocean.
Strange animals have
been found living at
great depths. They live
near cracks in the ocean

floor called volcanic vents. These animals never see the light of the sun. They get their energy from the heat of the volcanic vent.

Marine geologists are oceanographers who study mountains, rocks, and minerals in the ocean depths. They map the seafloor and drill for

Left: A technician inspects the flow of natural gas on an offshore drilling platform. Right: An oil-drilling rig in the Atlantic Ocean

deep sea mining

petroleum and natural gas. Mining of the seafloor for manganese nodules is a valuable resource for the future. Salt, manganese, and magnesium can also

Left: Core samples from Beaufort Sea, Alaska, stored in saltwater bins
Right: Studying a core sample from the bottom of Lake Erie to test for pollution

be taken from seawater
for our use.

Oceanographers also
drill core samples of the
seafloor. These are long,
tubelike sections of the
rock beneath the ocean
bottom. Such studies

helped prove that all the continents were once joined together and then drifted apart. This is called the theory of continental drift. Ships like the *Glomar Challenger* took part in these studies.

Other oceanographers study waves, tides, and currents as sources of energy. These may be used to turn turbines that generate electricity.

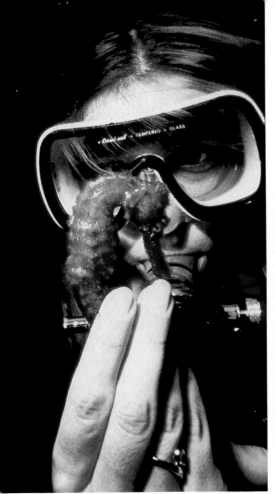

Left: A longsnout seahorse. Right: Rudderfish at Molokini Crater, Hawaii

Preserving the ocean environment is a major concern for the oceanographer. Problems that affect life in the oceans also affect life on land.

Left: Water pollution from a pumping station. Right: Workmen on a beach try to clean up oil that has leaked from an offshore oil well.

Most of Earth's oxygen is produced by microscopic creatures in the oceans. Oil spills and chemical pollution harm these creatures. Waste disposal and industrial use of

Left: Sea birds that have died in oil-polluted waters. Right: A poisonous oil spill off the coast of Mexico

water are other problems that oceanographers study.

Oceanographers sometimes work with meteorologists, or weather scientists. They have

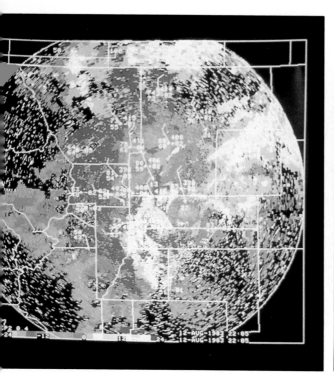

Scientists study weather information using radar-generated computer displays and charts.

learned much about how
the oceans affect our
weather. Their studies
have made it easier to
understand and forecast
our weather. Hurricanes
and tropical storms are

no longer as frightening as they once were, because they can be predicted more easily.

Sometimes even ocean currents can be destructive. There is a strong, warm current along the west coast of South America that can destroy marine life. It may also bring heavy rainfalls to some areas and

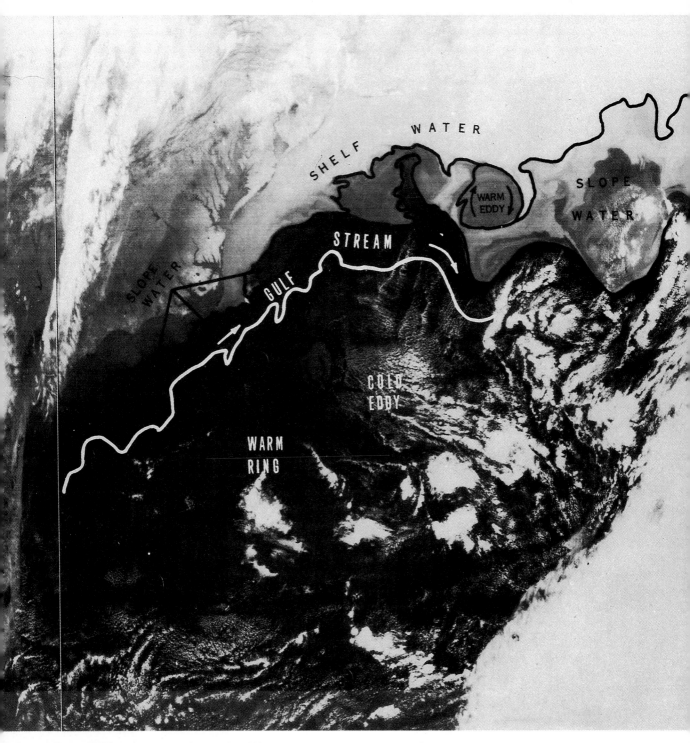

This satellite map shows the path of the
Atlantic Ocean current known as the Gulf Stream. Here its path is
outlined as it flows up the east coast of North America.

droughts to others. This current is called *El Niño* ("the child") because it generally occurs around the Christmas season.

Would you like to be an oceanographer? Oceanographers study all the physical, biological, geological, and chemical aspects of the sea. Almost any science can be applied to the study of the sea.

Above: A diver studying marine life in Hawaii. Below left: Model of an oil exploration and production center that would rest on the seafloor. Below right: A research vessel is lowered into the ocean from a ship operated by the Woods Hole Oceanographic Institution of Massachusetts.

To be an oceanographer you must study hard in mathematics and science. Read as many books as you can about marine life and Earth science. Perhaps someday you may be aboard a research vessel that makes the latest scientific discovery!

WORDS YOU SHOULD KNOW

atmosphere (AT • mus • fear)—the layers of air that surround the earth

biologist (by • OL • uh • jist)—a scientist who studies living creatures

continental drift (CON • ti • nen • tul DRIFT)—the theory that all the continents (large land masses) on Earth were once joined together and over millions of years have moved apart

core sample (KORE SAM • pul)—a tube-shaped section drilled out of rock, soil, or mud

echo sounder (EH • koe SOUND • er)—an instrument that measures the ocean's depth by sending out a sound wave and measuring its travel time

extinction (ex • TINK • shun)—the death of a whole species of creatures

food chain (FOOD CHAIN)—the system of larger animals depending on smaller animals for their food

geologist (jee • OL • uh • jist)—a scientist who studies rocks and minerals

interact (in • ter • ACT)—to act upon one another

krill (KRILL)—a tiny shellfish that is the major food of certain whales

marine (muh • REEN)—relating to the salt-water environment of the oceans

meteorologist (mee • tee • ur • OL • uh • jist)—a scientist who studies the weather

microscopic (my • kruh • SKOP • ic)—too tiny to be seen with the eyes; must be seen with a microscope

research vessel (REE • surch VES • ul)—a ship with scientific equipment for studying the ocean

sounding (SOUND • ing)—a test to see how deep the ocean is at a certain point

tides (TIDES)—the regular, daily rising and falling motions of the oceans

turbine (TUR • bin)—an engine that runs by the pressure of water, steam, or air

volcanic vent (vol • CAN • ik VENT)—the hole from which the steam or lava of a volcano comes out

INDEX

animals, sea, 12, 16-17
continental drift, 20
core samples, 19
currents, 20, 25-27
deep diving vessels, 8, 9, 16
Earth, 4, 5, 8, 22
echo sounder, 10-11
environment, ocean, 21-23
fish, 5, 6, 7, 12, 13, 14
fishing, 12, 15
food chain, 13
Glomar Challenger, 20
hunting, sea, 12
krill, 14-15
mammals, sea, 7, 12
marine biologists, 12, 16
marine geologists, 17-18
meteorologists, 23
mining, deep sea, 18-19

natural gas, 18
Niño, El, 27
ocean bottom, 9, 10-11, 16-17, 18-19
oceanographers, 5, 6, 8, 10-11, 12, 15, 19, 21, 23, 27, 29
oceans, 5, 6-7, 9, 10-11
petroleum, 18
plankton, 14-15
pollution, water, 22-23
research vessels, 8-9, 11, 29
sharks, 14
soundings, 10-11
tides, 5, 20
Trieste, 9
volcanic vents, 17
waves, 20
weather, 7, 23-25
whales, 14

PHOTO CREDITS

ABOUT THE AUTHOR

Paul Sipiera is an Associate Professor of Physical Sciences at William Rainey Harper College in Palatine, Illinois, and a research associate in geology at the Field Museum of Natural History in Chicago. As a member of the National Science Foundation's Antarctic Research Program, he has studied geological features of the icy continent. Mr. Sipiera is technical advisor to Society Expedition's Project Space Voyage, the first venture into space for the general public. A teacher of astronomy and geology, his specialties are meteorites, moon rocks, and volcanoes. Mr. Sipiera gardens, grows vegetables, and plants maples trees at his home in Crystal Lake, Illinois.